MW00743659

Join me
The Red Polka Dotted Pillow

To create an ideal setting
for positive change
and to ignite your passion

A place to hide

to heal

to access

your dreams, goals

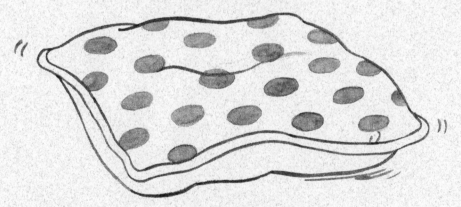

Hop aboard
The Mist–ical* Magical Pillow Awaits !

*One of the many SuZisms you'll discover   A perfect book for ages 15 to 115

Pillow Talk—Success Speaks

Susan Guild, motivator, innovator, poet and doodler, takes her fun seriously. Her poems are whimsical, lyrical, playful yet honest words to live by.

> – Louise Eastman, columnist, The Way I See It
> Medford, MA

The creative process is vital to survive on this planet.
> – Christina, Creative Healer, MFA
> Savannah, GA

The real you emerges out of the pillow and you.
> – Margo French, Chaplain, Scripps Memorial Hospital
> LaJolla, CA

The Red Polka Dotted Pillow is a brilliant book. It captures the essence of our inner playmate, our true selves – our very soul. Playing with this book will guide you to understanding what you truly desire and to manifesting magically.

> – Claudette Rowley, Personal and Professional Coach
> Lexington, MA

"Wake up your magic ladies and gentlemen" is my new motto: directly from Susan Guild. Her books, workbooks, and tools have become a light-hearted way to the real me. They are a joy to read and study. The Red Polka Dotted Pillow takes me forward from her other work in a most delightful thrilling process.

– Kay Wynne, CPA, Greentown Corners
   Virginia Beach, VA

Suz has taught me thru her books, workshops and mostly thru The Red Polka Dotted Pillow how to see what has been underneath my shell for so many years. My dreams are now coming true.

– Joanne Hight, TC, Artist and Teacher
   Rowley, MA

Just what I needed and more. Suz's workshops, poetry and exercises creatively guide you to your inner magical self. The creative arts process she uses is fun, creative and gently nudges you step by step to focus on your dreams. Commit yourself and experience amazing results.

– Sandi Forman, Training Specialist
   Boston, MA

A Wake Up Your Magic™ Book

Copyright 2004
All Rights Reserved
ISBN #0-9667545-3-0

Published by
Wish Publications
c/o Guild House
Winchester, MA 01890

The Red Polka Dotted Pillow

Wake Up The Real Who Within You

Susan C. Guild

Book and cover illustrations by Judy Huber

Mary Gal
May you feel
inspired to
succeed to
places w/
this Book
w/ luv
Sue

Table of Contents

Poem	Activity	Pages
Little Flower of Bloom	A New Beginning	1–6
Oh, Where Oh Where Am I going	Question – Ask	7–13
Deserving	Move Out Beyond the Shadows	14–18
Creativity	Celebrate the Real Who Within You	19–23
The Upside Down Heart	Listen Within	24–29
Call Back Your Energy	Surrender to the Divine Within	30–34
The Ship of Joy	Adventure into the Unknown	35–41
Inner Peace	Climb Towards De-light	42–46
Freedom	Fly With Your Dreams	47–52
The Sacred Circle	Manifest Gifts Beyond Belief	53–58
The Vow	Create the Wedding Within	59–64
The Red Polka Dotted Pillow	Discover the Power of the Mist–ical Magical Pillow	65–69

This book is dedicated to my inner play-mate

An ode to me

A gift beyond belief

This is my inner being
always flowing pure positive energy
always by my side
ready to connect when called upon in joy
ready to disconnect when in fear
anger, blame or being coy
the benefits, dear one, of pure
positive energy are extraordinaire
tho can be easily ordinaire

continue

1

Yes, the energy flows
The stress goes
The immune, the endocrine systems build
Endorphins swirl ~ you feel on a whirl
Cells revitalize, circulation is tip top
You increasingly smile from the inside out
Your complexion improves ~ just what you sought
So inner play-mate
Thank you ~ thank you
Always there, ready to assist
Not willing to resist
You are my core, my life force, my essence

Your inner play-mate is the true who within you !

Purpose

This is a gentle healing book to

    awaken ~ access ~ actualize your dreams, your goals

        to trust the wisdom of your inner play-mate

            that voice within ~ to be used alone ~ in a group

                or as a teaching tool

Yes, yes, yes
Get in touch with me
Your true self
Your inner core
Then
And only then
can your dreams
your goals come true !

Your Inner Being

Suggested use

Enjoy the book as a poetry book.

Read each poem and then complete
the correlating activity after
each poem. Exercises are identified
with action verbs.

Create your own Wake Up Your Magic™ book circle.
Determine how best to use the book,
either professionally or personally.
Read as a whole or divide in segments.

Read aloud ~ read silently ~ create

sew ~ move ~ paint ~ color
day by day, step by step. Have fun with it
to discover your vision, your truth,
your accountability to self.

From the author

Today I have a blank page of endless possibilities, probabilities

What choices do I choose

What pen or brush do I pick up

Do I stay in the shoulds ~ the coulds ~ trying

Or

Take the risk

Ask...ask...ask again

For the courage

The openness

To share once again

Another Wake Up Your Magic™ book

The power of the Red Polka Dotted Pillow

To draw out the radiance ~ the wholeness within you

To allow your dreams ~ your goals to bubble up inside you ~ to flow

Through words, images, symbols onto the paper

Your inner play-mate awaits

Start now !

Little Flower Of Bloom

A New Beginning

Little Flower Of Bloom

Are you speaking to me
Little flower of bloom
And what pray tell do you say
This fine day
I hear
I just hear
The 'ole' ways just ain't working
So they say
'tis time to loosen the reins
to let go of the horse
the carriage
the back pack
the days of no roads

continue

2

Yes, new paths ~ new choices
Are upon us
This fine day
The 'ole' ways just ain't working
So they say
'Tis time to put us in that mode
Of faith ~ of trust
Stop ~ hear me
This blooming flower within
Hear the voice from the
Inside out
Hear what it has to say
Let go of the reins
Find your own path
Yes, there is so much more
More than we can comprehend
From sunrise to sunset

Psssst
O Listen....

continue

3

Once we listen ~ once we hear
Pay attention
So may your flower of bloom
Speak out
Be heard
May yours blossom ~ bud
From
Seedling to sprout
Yes, this day has so much in store
For us
Once we hear the flower
See the light
On this fine day
This day
The day
Your day !

Plant the Seeds of Greatness

Let this book come alive as you play, paint, add texture and color everywhere ~ anywhere.

May these words set the tone for you the reader
as you turn the pages ~ inner-act with verse
explore activities.
May you feel ~ see ~ hear the light
as you dance with your inner play-mate ~ the voice from the inside out
longing to be heard.
Let the magic begin !

My Play-mate's Name
Suzette

Author SuZ's inner play-mate's name is SuZette. For Suz, SuZette is delightful to chat with, listen to her guidance, write letters to and more.

"Art is the imagination at play in the field of time. Let yourself play."
—Julia Cameron, The Artists' Way

Commit Now

Within each of us lies
Hidden dreams
Shadows
Lurking to emerge
While
All the while
That inner play-mate
Our child like persona
Of years gone by
Is pulling at our sleeves
Go for it
Go for it !

Let me, your inner play-mate, your inner being, be limitless, light and free to guide you on your path.

commit to stay with this book.

I, now_____
(your inner play-mate name here)

Date: _____
(today's)

Signature_____

6

Oh, Where Oh Where Am I Going

Question ~ Ask

Oh, Where Oh Where Am I Going

Oh, where oh where am I going

And

What am I willing to take

It feels like time ~ yes, time

To get on with it

The sowing

The mowing

To get out the tools

To look

At who I really am

To pick up the shovel and the rake

continue

To ask

1. Who am I

2. Where am I going

3. What action am I willing to take

Wow

This action ~ this action

Could it be true for little 'ole' me

To pick up my flag ~ my staff of life

To remember

To understand

Whatever we vibrate right now

We get back

We attract the perfect match

continue

9

So sing
Chant
Hum
Matchmaker matchmaker
Open the doors
Unlock the hatch
Let in the perfect match !

With no time to think, quickly jot down 57 dreams,
goals (let them emerge out of nowhere) for this lifetime ! Begin here

1. _____

"Keep writing—Often the best comes when
you open your mind and go deeper. It could be
number 37 or 42 or 51."
                    —Mark LeBlanc, Small Business Success

continue

More more to expand – to explore !

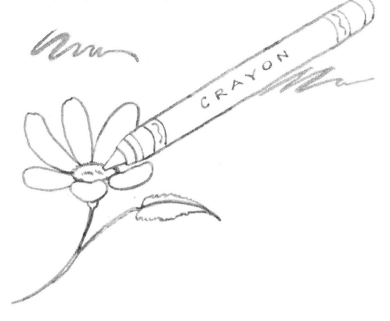

Let them flow
everything and
anything is acceptable.

56. ————
57. ————

"Imagination is more important than knowledge."
—Albert Einstein

Ponder... Think... Feel

Every day this week, answer these questions

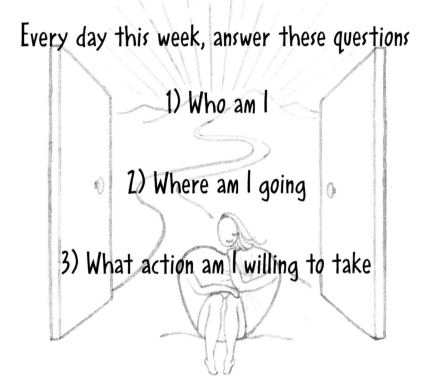

1) Who am I

2) Where am I going

3) What action am I willing to take

When one door closes

Two more open wise

Magnified straight from the heart

Right in front of your eyes

"If you are clear about what you want, the world responds with clarity."
—Loretta Stark

13

Deserving

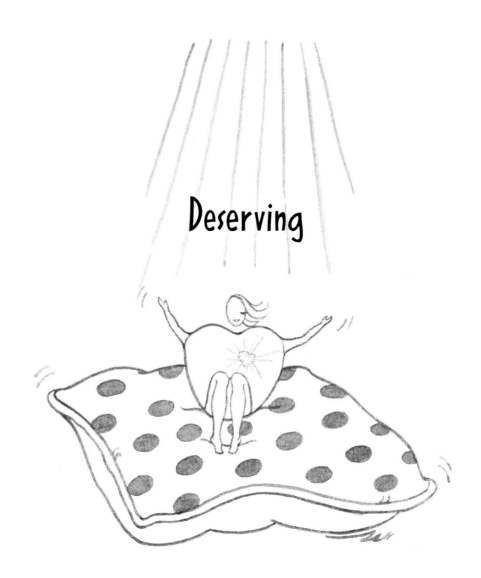

Move Beyond the Shadows

Deserving

Is it deserving or constantly swerving
Can we go beyond the deeply
Etched shadows
Answer the real questions
Lurking below the surface
Or
Are we content with the gloss
The newly applied varnish ~ the floss
Or
Can we take out the sandpaper
Go underneath
For the real shine
Wow wee
What a relief ~ what a find

continue

15

Can we live each day
Fully as kings and queens
Savoring today's sweetness
Rather than
Munching on yesterday's cake
Delving into the full expression
Of joy
Clarifying ~ focusing
Our vision, our goal
Exploring ~ pursuing
Our true essence of soul

Pretending to have it all together
What a habit
What a fake

continue

Deserving
Can be our prayer
To go forth
Un-nerving
To stop swerving
Daring to be adventuresome, courageous and bold
Going beyond superficial understanding
What a hold
This is my prayer ~ my ode
To do it
To say it
To be it

Deserve it ~ decree it ~ and it must be !

Paint... Punch... Probe

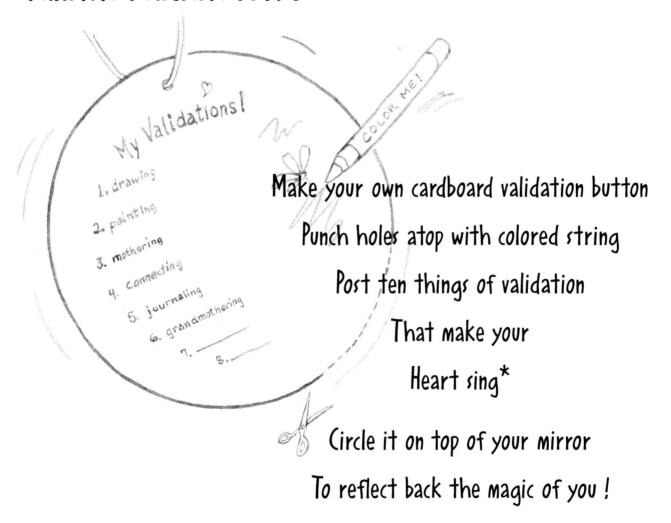

My Validations!

1. drawing
2. painting
3. mothering
4. connecting
5. journaling
6. grandmothering
7. _____
8. _____

COLOR ME!

Make your own cardboard validation button

Punch holes atop with colored string

Post ten things of validation

That make your

Heart sing*

Circle it on top of your mirror

To reflect back the magic of you !

*in memory of Subway Sam
(my friend Bill Linkow)

"We teach people how to treat us. When you don't believe in yourself, you communicate that to everyone around you."
— Phillip C. McGraw, PhD (Dr. Phil)

Creativity

Celebrate the Real Who Within You

Creativity

Creativity heals ~ squeals ~ reveals

Creativity inspires

Ignites the fires

Creativity makes the energy flow

Keeps us healthy, on the go

Creativity

Erases loneliness ~ blame ~ hurt

Energizes ~strengthens ~clarifies

Keeps us from being curt

Creativity begets inspiration

Not vegetation

continue

Creativity manifests silent power

Waiting to bloom like a gorgeous flower

Creativity acts as a token

To

The subway of the mind

So when you are stuck

Knee deep in the muck

When you are in total doubt

Ready to pout

Reach for the paint brush

Not the phone

Reach For Me

Journal To Color & Doodle

continue

Change your mood
Create a new perspective
Let creativity be your quick fix
Dust off the caps of paint of vivid color
Then
Yellar
Wow wee
I'm ready
I'm ready
To
Wake up
That
Real me within me !

Celebrate the Spirit Within

Color Me!

Stuff it with self love

Strength and courage

Decorate it with beads

Buttons ~ colorful fabric

Place it on your Red Polka Dotted Pillow

Make it a constant reminder to

Cherish, trust, honor you

Listen to your dialogue within

Your

Inner play-mate

Your Wake Up Your Magic™ doll awaits !

"Creativity is celebrating the spirit within."
—Author Suz (that's me !)

23

The Upside Down Heart

Listen Within

The Upside Down Heart

Leap with it ~ play with it
Honor it
Trust it
Your heart is speaking ~ are you listening

Is your heart upside down
Are you walking on your hands
Or
Is it sideways ~ are you walking
On your elbows
Is it filled with fear
Anger ~ blame
From fear comes insight ~ not shame

continue

25

So face it ~ heal it
Throw out those crutches
Don't be lame
Put pep back in your step
Rekindle the vim ~ vigor ~ of the soul
Fill up that empty hole

Yes
Meditate twice daily ~ jot down messages gaily
Take a class ~ toast your glass
Be your own inner healer
Your body's wheeler dealer
Clean out your closets ~ the closets of your mind
Oh ~ what a find

continue

Yes, the scales have tipped
The fight is gone
The heart is back
Leap with it ~ trust it ~ play with it
Your heart is speaking
Are you listening
The heart is full
Pulsating ~ strong

A chalice of love
The resurrection of spirit !

Leap… Play…Trust

"Once you are present in your own heart

you find yourself going places your mind never dreamt of."
—Martha Beck, Life Coach

Your heart is speaking

Are you listening

This week take a leap of faith ~ go for it !

continue

Feel... See... Hear

I am proud of me because
_____
_____

I appreciate you (my pals) because
_____
_____

As seen thru the eyes of the heart

Make them

Draw them

Color them

Paint them

Punch them

Tie with purple ribbon

Fill with appreciation* of yourself

Fill with appreciation* of those

Close to you

Wear them ~ dance with them over your heart !

*Appreciation turns up your heart again and again !

"Even If you are on the right path, you get run over if you just sit there."

—Will Rogers

Call Back Your Energy

Surrender to the Divine Within

Call Back Your Energy

partner

workplace

children

carpool I call back my energy with glee

To those I gave it all to

friends

volunteer

Yes, of course

I'll do anything ~ of course, me

No matter what I need or felt

PTA

At

Your beck and call was I

'Call back your energy'

She says

Fill my body

With the light of gold

With loving consciousness

With the power of one-ness

What a great way to take hold

continue

Of course, you are right
It makes no difference my feelings
Of course, I was sick, depleted and tired
Cuz everybody else's energy was mired
Yes ~ better to please
To listen to the authority
The family ~ the hired

Than re-claim me
So
Good-bye
To
Dis-ease ~ fear ~ resistance

fear
resistance
dis-ease

reclaim me!
personal power
lifeforce

continue

Instead I fill my body ~ aura with light
I surrender to the divine within
I let go ~ let go
Sense my own direction
Drive my own bus
Continue life with
Such robust

Having a ball on the path of joy
Eating everything including bok choy !

Joy↑

Create... Individualize

When your personal truths match your universal truths you're soaring

Create your own personal ritual to call back your energy !

1. Write down your plan.

2. Bring accessories you need — i.e. candles, incense, rocks, paints, pine cones whatever speaks to you.

3. Set aside your own private time — make a contract with yourself and do it.

Innovate before it's too late
Make a call back your energy altar.

"Every day in every way
I am getting better and better."
—Emil Cové

The Ship Of Joy

Adventure into the Unknown

The Ship Of Joy

We blame

We analyze

We discuss

We disgust

We frustrate

We mistake

We cry ~ we why ~ we fly

Finally we laugh ~ light those fires

Wake up our secret passions ~ those hidden desires

We discover the contrast

Of the no – no – no's

Navigate us towards

Exhilarating ho – ho – ho's

Ho

Ho

Ho

No

No

No

continue

We pull up the anchor
Clean the center board
Take hold of the rudder
We surrender to the process ~ we hop aboard

We affirm ~ we confirm
300 times
not
30
Play straight now ... no cheating
No playing dirty
We forgive
We release
We accept
The who or what that makes
Us feel hurt-y

continue

We learn again ~ it's time to begin
The ship awaits
Casts a spell for new destinations
A
Mist-ical ~ magical
Win
The tide has turned
The captain is back
Ready to embark ~ safely depart

The ship awaits
The ship ahoy
The ship of joy !

"I'm no longer afraid of storms,
for I am learning how to sail my own ship."

–Louisa May Alcott

I get it

Release... Release... Release

Written in thick green magic marker is really healing

Today I _____ release
forgive, accept, _____
(the who or what bugging me)
for things real or imagined.

I now ask the _____ to forgive me.
(the who or what)

I now forgive, release, accept
me — yes me
from the _____.
(the who or what which was bugging me)

300 times not 30

Post this where you'll see it — i.e. bathroom mirror, file cabinet, car dashboard.

"Strongly held negative emotions alter
the chemistry of the body causing disease."
—Catherine Ponder, Dynamic Laws of Healing

Sailing Anew

Today I _____
(your inner play-mate's name)

massage my heart with a new

sense of inner

soul-full joy. I release 'ole'

stagnant anger, pain and guilt so

I no longer attract that to me.

human garbage
compactor
layer after layer
ole habits, beliefs, behaviors

"What we suppress, our bodies express."
—Barbara Ganin, Art and Healing
Using Expressive Arts to Heal
Mind, Body and Spirit

Inner Peace

Climb Towards De – Light

Inner Peace

Up, up and away
Do we run, do we stray
Or
Do we come back home to the real connection
The soul ~ the inner core
Where we can play
Relinquish ~ release ~ revive
Go for more
Take off that heavy fur coat
Unbuckle the stroller of years before
Let out that inner kid again
Be one with one
With others ~ with spirit
Clean out your ears
Listen ~ witness ~ hear it

continue

Create those stairs of inner peace

Start now; your inner play-mate awaits
Design ten steps
Fill with color ~ taste ~ texture
Saturate with de-light
What a special way to
Start your flight
For #1 jot down your gifts
For #2 compose some exotic dates

3.

'Tis your time ~ just for you
Not Ms. Sally or Sue

2. compose exotic dates

1. my gifts

continue ⇒

Now on up to # 5 ~ iron out
Pressing problems
What a pun ~ oh what fun
Then up to # 10
Once you begin ~ it's easy to pretend
Yes, the climb gets easier
The beam gets brighter
The healing stronger
You count ~ your feelings count
Your soul counts
You
The lover ~ the dancer ~ the poet of life
Ascending
Up, up and away
To the real connection
Designing your dreams
Deep within the crevice of the soul !

Design Your Heart Steps

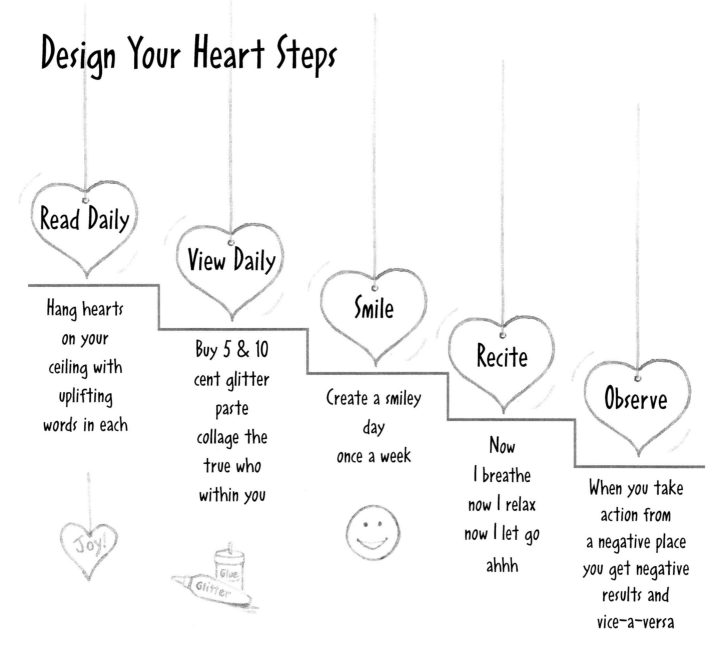

Read Daily

Hang hearts on your ceiling with uplifting words in each

Joy!

View Daily

Buy 5 & 10 cent glitter paste collage the true who within you

Glue Glitter

Smile

Create a smiley day once a week

Recite

Now I breathe now I relax now I let go ahhh

Observe

When you take action from a negative place you get negative results and vice-a-versa

"The greatest danger for most of us is not our aim is too high and we miss it, but it is too low and we reach it."
—Michelangelo

Then on to step *10...

Freedom

Fly with Your Dreams

Freedom

Is it the first amendment or
Walking on the beach with the wind blowing in your hair
Or is it moving out beyond feeling
Liberated ~ uncaged
Finding your own obtainable reach
So why do we, this enlightened species
Continue to hold in bondage
Those we love ~ they come closer
We hold on tight ~ blame ~ connive
Strangle ~ suffocate ~shove
We finish the story
Before
It starts

continue

We act it out
Send out weird vibes
Undermine extraordinary friendships
Congeniality ~ good will
Can anybody tell us the whys
We know ~ we all know
It works so very well when
We relinquish being general manager of the universe
We let back in the excitement
The gusto of life
We give up the hearse
So why not let spirit, our inner play-mate
Guide us on this one
And the bonus to boot is the ultimate dessert
That's soooo perfect ~ soooo fun

continue

So what's freedom
Can we feel uncaged, liberated
Move out ~ beyond
Hold on to this state
The vibration of freedom
Then, and only then ~ ask our questions
Make our decisions
Trip the light fantastic
Footloose and fancy free
Dance confidently
Boldly ~ fearlessly
Up the avenue of life
Eating
Yogurt and ghee !

Draw... Dance... Move

Freedom is speaking through your body

I _____ stop holding
(real name)

on so tight — trying to control outcomes.
I honestly release being general manager of the universe.

This week notice tight spots
in your body. Draw them,
access and acknowledge them.
Then, wow, have fun with
this. Mindfully act out
your desired physical sensations
of freedom — of flow — of movement !

*Massaging your head
and feet is fun, too*

"Mindfulness...means conscious awareness
of all of faculties...ourselves."
—Anne Glusker, Oprah Magazine, 5/01

Magic... Magic... Magic

Do not
disturb
universe at
work

Magic is in the air when . . .

I _____ stop looking for
(inner play-mate's name)

_____
(the who or what I'm yearning for)

and trust it, in whatever form is best, _____ will
(the who or what)

come into my life — that's freedom !

For more magic,
paint page a
bright color
sprinkle with
fairy dust

"You are what you think about."
—Earl Nightengale

The Sacred Circle

Manifest Gifts Beyond Belief

The Circle

The circle ~ the circle

The joining together

The ring of wellness

The spiral of wholeness

The co-creating

The tool ~ the technique ~ the catalyst

To unleash

Talents ~ gifts ~ potential

The circle ~ the circle

The pulsing of the heart

The beating of the drum

The opening of the soul

The march of the butterfly

Soft-gentle ~ colorful ~ whole

continue

The birthing back to authenticity
To
Spirit
Sensuality
Silly~ness
Still~ness
That unique space within
Not laced with sin or gin
Yes, the time is right to let your butterfly take flight
Find ~ form ~ follow
Your own sacred circle
The circle
Meet regularly
Make the Red Polka Dotted Pillow
Your mascot
See it ~ do it
Be it

continue

Experience this book

Step by step ~ week by week
Poem by poem ~ exercise by exercise
Commit
Commit
Then commit again

To manifest your dreams ~ your goals
Stashed under
The Red Polka Dotted Pillow

For gifts beyond belief!

Write... Gather... Attract

Appreciation Circle

It is my hope, my dream that you form your own circle, the Wake Up Your Magic™ circle and do all my books. Name a facilitator and let the circles ripple out with each member starting another circle.

Write all the things you appreciate about your enemies and friends 'til their light shines through in circles on a huge piece of paper !

Cherish Circle

Gather your friends. Have each tell what you cherish about each other clockwise and counterclockwise in a circle !

Attraction Circle

Surround yourself with fun people and you'll be fun and so much more !

"Out of play comes the vision–the de-light, the dream–the goal !"
—author Suz (that's me !)

Sewing Circle

Your pillow
The pillow
Your mascot

self-respect

joy

commitment

joy   joy

loyalty

joy

joy

Make this pillow

Stuff it with commitment

Loyalty and self respect

Seal with trust . . . use white shimmery satin – sew or glue on

red felt dots

The power of the Red Polka Dotted Pillow has come alive

Bind with lace and elegance – seal with authenticity !

"Wake each morning with the thought, something wonderful is about to happen."
—Flavio

The Vow

Create the Wedding Within

The Vow

The vow ~ the vow
The giving of self to self
The marriage of one
This is a must
The marriage ~ the love affair of
Me to me
Of
You to you
The wholeness ~ the oneness
The celebration
To love
To nurture
To cherish
To trust

continue

'Til death do me part
'Til hell freezes over
Flaking its crust
This is it guys
My own personal wedding
Of moi to moi
The ritual ~ the pageantry
The candles ~ the stars
The softness ~ the light
The truth of our being
The signing of a new lease
The time is here ~ the day is now
To
Create ~ recite
Make up ~ perform ~ by self

continue

61

Whatever it takes
maybe even on the sand
your personalized rite
the vow
dress up ~ a veil ~ a top hat
Boutonnière ~ music ~ flowers
maybe even a cat
ask ~ expect ~ intend ~ believe
the ultimate love affair
the power of one
the power of loving
and
it must be !

The Vow

Ask... Ask... Ask

Before writing your vow ask:

AM I...

Goals & Dreams

Honest with what I truly want

Or is it what others want for me

Or what others say, think, control or say

Or what I do for approval, praise or support

I _____ now write my vow ~ WOW

(inner play-mate's name)

This works best when you make four columns on a large sheet of paper and you list

all your dreams and goals ~ then and only then

you check off each idea !

"We must be willing to get rid of the life we've
planned, so as to have the life that is waiting."
—Joseph Campbell

Decorate... Declare

The Marriage Vow

I _____ do solemnly swear
(your name)

pledge ~ affirm to honor ~ to trust ~ to obey _____
(inner play-mate's name)

to love ~ to cherish ~ to nurture _____
(inner play-mate's name)

to _____ .
(what I truly want)

Marital instructions:
Write or paste this on poster
board ~ recite your private ceremony.
Hang with a decorated clothes pin on closet
door to be read again and again !

Date _____
Signature _____

"Man's main task is to give birth to himself."
—Erich Fromm, psychoanalyst and sociologist

The Red Polka Dotted Pillow

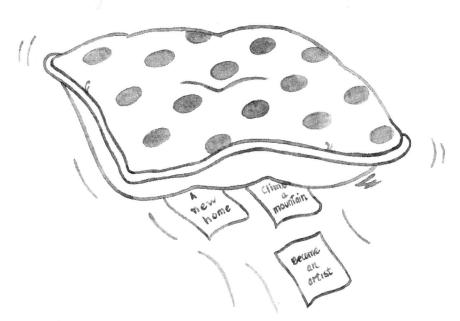

The Power of the Mist-ical ~ Magical Pillow

The Red Polka Dotted Pillow

Know it ~ say it
Do it ~ be it
If not now ~ when

Dust off those thoughts ~ fantasies
Put them under the Red Polka Dotted Pillow
Sleep well
Ask ~ ask ~ ask for guidance
Go for more
Can we honestly say

Asleep or awake
I know ~ I know ~ I know
Can we honestly answer

continue

66

This I know ~ I know ~ I just know
Who I am
And
What I am
The who and the what
Is this it
A perfect fit
I know ~ I just know
I am a mortal on this earth
Running along side the path
Not on it
Confused ~ afraid ~ naked ~ great
With the vim and
Vigor of a marathon
Runner trying to lose weight

continue

Though when I stop

Look ~ listen

The cats and dogs cease fighting inside

No longer do I need to march upstairs

With everything covered

Including my hide

Can we finally bare our soul

To say

This is it ~ the perfect fit

With no forcing ~ controlling or pushing

This process ~ this oneness

With such immense power

Bigger

Than any mortal on earth

Creates

Manifests

Lets the miracles happen !

Now Showing

The Red Polka Dotted Pillow

You are the producer, director

and designer so

Don't walk out of the theatre

In the dark ~ in a funk

Instead create your own life's script

Light the lights ~ full of spunk !

My Life Script

created & directed by ME!

The Power of the Red Polka Dotted Pillow Has Spoken !

"Those who can see the invisible can do the impossible."
— Carl Mays, President, Creative Living

69

In Conclusion

As you romped

and scampered

Thru the pages with your

Infamous inner play-mate

May you have connected with something

So special ~ so extraordinaire

To

Mirror the real who within you

To

Bring forth a passion you've forgotten

May you understand the contrast of the ho ho ho's *

That when something absolutely

Does not work like the broken record

Going round and round with no return

* Ship of Joy poem

VI

continue

You return to

The pages of the Red Polka Dotted Pillow

To

Focus on what works for you

To

Be truly aligned with your inner play-mate

With such de-light

always ~ yet always

Reaching for the light

to be read

again and again

Hey
I am this blooming flower within
color me deliciously
grateful

LuV
SuZ

"I would have my ears filled with the world's music.
Let me hear all sounds of life and living."

– Maya Angelou

VII

Billows and Pillows of Love and Support

Many thanks to those who
gently pushed and prodded me
to bring out my own dreams and wishes
and
tap my inner play-mate within !

Linda Guild
for doing the last edit

My loyal awesome classes
who week by week
proved the power of
creative expression

Carolyn Ford
for her insistence on using the
inner play-mate

PJ for her
extraordinary
patience of my
creative mind and her
computer knowledge

Alison Huber
for transcribing the
final manuscript and technical
help

Joseph for stepping in and saving
the day with his graphic design
expertise

Laura Guild for
typing the original manuscript

Evana
my dear, loyal friend

continue

Many thanks continued

Judy Huber, an artist, teacher and Reiki Master walking her own healing path, is a natural for this book. Her drawings capture her belief in her own inner play-mate, creating them through the meditative process. Her studio, alive with children/adult art and Reiki classes over the years, has been a place of inspiration for book illustrations. Here you will find Judy and her inner play-mate splashing joyfully in watercolor. She lives in Kingston, NH with her husband Dennis, has two children, Dan and Alison and one grandchild, Shayla She may be reached at 603 642-8346

Claudette Rowley
for the reminder to stand
in my magnificence

Marcel for his patient
support and intuitive insights

Dick
for copy material

Christie Cummings
for her
creative coaching

Sue Giaimo, Deede and Glenn
for believing in me

SuZ's Epilogue

We are living in very special exciting times where the energy has sped up. Things manifest easily, effortlessly according to our vibrational and emotional energies. The Red Polka Dotted Pillow takes you on a journey of hope, of faith following your own inner star, your true source.

Substantial evidence and research now prove the validation of creative expression, used in many areas of this book, the Mist-ical-Magical pillow ride:

*Play-fullness allows us to access our true spirit in a whole new way, a new state of being an authentic Mind, Body, Spirit healing.

*Therapists, over and over, recommend replacing an addiction and/or chronic illness's fear and confusion with focus, the intent of passion, aliveness and joy.

*Creative art play is a tool to change rigid stuck patterns of the brain's left side according to recent Neurobiology studies.

*Expressive Arts is now a popular college major for students, therapists, school counselors, and health professionals. Expressive Arts allows freedom and flexibility in your own choices for facilitating change.

*Putting pen to paper activates a part of your brain, the Reticular Activating System, to activate the real who within you.

*The Sacred Circle renews, restores, rejuvenates us with community and camaraderie in this highly technological and impersonal world today.

continue

X

Step out. Form your own creativity circle – the Wake Up Your Magic™ circle. Walk the journey of my other books, Wake Up Your Magic, Find Your Dancing Heart, and this, The Red Polka Dotted Pillow. Journal, write, draw, decorate, act, play. Create with a group or individually day by day, step by step. My classes thrive on this.

Your inner play-mate awaits. Personal life fulfillment awaits. Increased vitality awaits.
More joy awaits.
Shine bright. Follow your own inner star. This is my journey, my inner vision, my path to higher awareness.
Use this book to help determine yours.

Feel free to contact me as you awaken, as you celebrate, the real who within you !

Susan C. Guild
www.wakeupyourmagic.com
suzguild@mac.com

Order Form

Quantity	Product	Price	Total
	Wake Up Your Magic Book	$13^{99}	
	Find Your Dancing Heart Book	$16^{99}	
	The Red Polka Dotted Pillow Book	$18^{99}	
	Magical Combo: Wake Up Your Magic and Find Your Dancing Heart Book	$28^{99}	
	Adult Inspirational Kit: Wake Up Your Magic Book, memo pad, and Crayola® colored pencils	$17^{50}	
	100 Sheet Magnetized Memo Pad	$6^{99}	
	4 Inspirational Sayings Memo Pad	$5^{99}	
	Color-Me-Happy Variety Postcard Packet	$5^{99}	
		Sub-total	
		Tax	
		Shipping	
		Total	

Make checks payable to and send to:
Wake Up Your Magic Enterprises
38 Church Street Winchester, MA 01890
Phone: 781-729-6928 Fax: 781-729-6928
www.wakeupyourmagic.com

Company/Store/Your Name _____

Address & Phone/Fax_____

E-mail_____

Customer Signature_____

Call or e-mail for Wake Up Your Magic™ professional workshops or presentations. Bulk and wholesale orders welcome.

suzguild@mac.com